BRITISH RAILWAY
TICKETS

Jan Dobrzynski

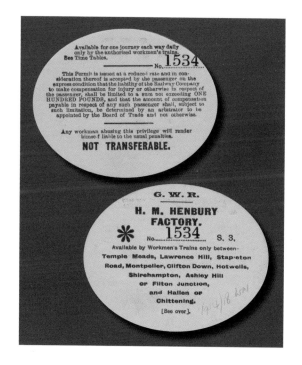

SHIRE PUBLICATIONS

Published in Great Britain in 2011 by Shire Publications Ltd, Midland House, West Way, Botley, Oxford OX2 0PH, United Kingdom.

44-02 23rd Street, Suite 219, Long Island City, NY 11101, USA.

E-mail: shire@shirebooks.co.uk   www.shirebooks.co.uk

© 2011 Jan Dobrzynski.

Every attempt has been made by the Publishers to secure the appropriate permissions for materials reproduced in this book. If there has been any oversight we will be happy to rectify the situation and a written submission should be made to the Publishers.

A CIP catalogue record for this book is available from the British Library.

Shire Library no. 637.   ISBN-13: 978 0 74780 844 2

Jan Dobrzynski has asserted his right under the Copyright, Designs and Patents Act, 1988, to be identified as the author of this book.

Designed by Tony Truscott Designs, Sussex, UK and typeset in Perpetua and Gill Sans.

Printed in China through Worldprint Ltd.

11 12 13 14 15   10 9 8 7 6 5 4 3 2 1

COVER IMAGE
A selection of railway tickets from a collection.

TITLE PAGE IMAGE
The two sides of an unusual oval-shaped GWR workman's ticket.

CONTENTS PAGE IMAGE
The front and back of George Stephenson's personal Stockton & Darlington Railway ivory button ticket.

EDITOR'S NOTE
Please note that tickets in the book are not all shown at the same scales, and that most are shown somewhat smaller than the originals.

ACKNOWLEDGEMENTS
I should like to thank Elizabeth and Michael Stewart for permission to copy and reproduce tickets from their collection, and also David Geldard, John Hawkins and Keith Turner for their expert advice, guidance and use of material from their collections. I gratefully acknowledge the support and assistance of Ian Bolton of Birmingham Central Library for facilitating the use of the extensive Wingate H. Bett transport ticket collection and for permission to use illustrations of tickets reproduced in this book. I would also like to thank fellow collectors and dealers and the Transport Ticket Society for their help and assistance. In addition my thanks go to staff and volunteers of the Severn Valley Railway and to employees of train operating company London Midland for taking time from their duties to help with photography.

Images of tickets and other illustrations are acknowledged as follows:

John Hawkins: pages 10, 20(top), 21(middle left), 22(top left), 35(2nd top left), 40, 41(bottom right), 42, 43(top & bottom), 49(middle);

Reproduced from the Railway Special Collection, with the permission of Birmingham Libraries and Archives: pages 6, 7 (top 2nd down), 12 (middle), 17 (middle), 20 (bottom), 21 (top middle right and bottom), 23, 27, 34 (top), 37, 45, 46 (bottom), 47 (bottom), 48 (bottom), 49 (bottom), 58 (top and middle), 60 (middle and bottom), 61 (bottom 2 rows), 62;

Michael and Elizabeth Stewart: pages 1, 3, 4, 7 (top), 8, 11 (top and middle), 16 (bottom), 17 (top and bottom), 24 (middle), 28 (top), 32, 33, 36, 41 (left) 68 (bottom).

Keith Turner [insert] 11 (bottom).

All other photographs are from the author's collection

Shire Publications is supporting the Woodland Trust, the UK's leading woodland conservation charity, by funding the dedication of trees.

CONTENTS

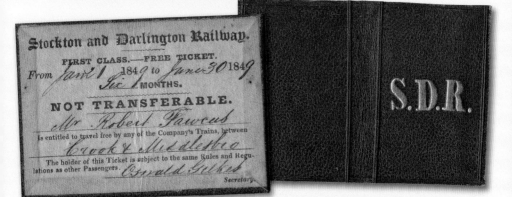

Opening

OF

THE LIVERPOOL AND MANCHESTER

RAILWAY,

WEDNESDAY, 15TH SEPTEMBER, 1830.

CHAS. LAWRENCE, CHAIRMAN.

THE BEARER OF THIS TICKET IS ENTITLED TO SEAT No. *53.*

NORTH STAR'S TRAIN.

ENT*d. T. Read*

YELLOW FLAG.

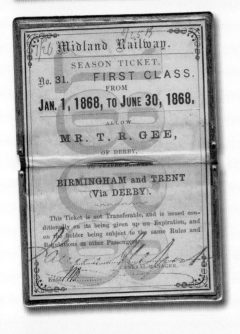

Stockton and Darlington Railway.

FIRST CLASS.—FREE TICKET.

From *Jan 1* 184*9* to *June 30* 184*9*

Six MONTHS.

NOT TRANSFERABLE.

Mr Robert Fawcus

Is entitled to travel free by any of the Company's Trains, between

Crook & Middlesbro

The holder of this Ticket is subject to the same Rules and Regulations as other Passengers. *Oswald Silkes*

Secretary.

S.D.R.

Midland Railway.

SEASON TICKET.

No. 31. FIRST CLASS.

FROM

JAN. 1, 1868, TO JUNE 30, 1868.

ALLOW

MR. T. R. GEE,

OF DERBY,

TO TRAVEL BETWEEN

BIRMINGHAM and TRENT

(Via DERBY).

This Ticket is not Transferable, and is issued conditionally on its being given up on Expiration, and on the holder being subject to the same Rules and Regulations as other Passengers.

GENERAL MANAGER.

MIDLAND RAILWAY

INTRODUCTION

THE BRITISH RAILWAY TICKET has its origins in a time before railway transport became widespread, in the late eighteenth and early nineteenth centuries, when the horse-drawn stagecoach was the main form of public transport in the British Isles, and other modes of travel included ships and boats that plied coastal waters or rivers and canals. The overland stagecoach network stretched over thousands of miles of turnpike roads, serving most principal cities, towns and villages and calling at coaching inns at intervals of approximately 10 miles, where the horses would be changed for a fresh team, and passengers could find rest and refreshment. Tens of thousands of horses were maintained, and thousands of people made a living serving the needs of a relatively small number of passengers.

Stagecoach travel was arduous, uncomfortable and hazardous. Many roads were in poor condition and became impassable during severe weather, and so delays were common. Accidents were frequent and highway robbery was another danger. A speedier and more secure coaching service was offered by the Royal Mail, which ran through the night. The mail coach, in the charge of a driver and a heavily armed guard, carried two classes of passenger, the

Opposite:
The top ticket was something new when it was issued on the opening day of the Liverpool & Manchester Railway. Two decades later, tickets and passes had become as commonplace as the railways themselves. The lower two passes are shown next to their outer covers.

Left: Opened on 27 September 1825, the Stockton & Darlington Railway established steam traction for the transport of goods and passengers, but tickets were not used by passengers during the early years.

5

This slightly charred stagecoach waybill from the North British Railway was rescued from a station-yard bonfire, along with the tickets below.

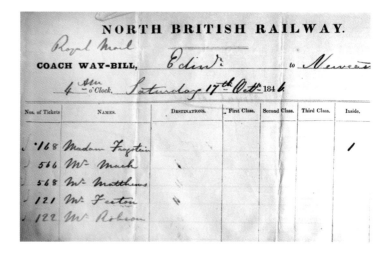

Tickets printed by Gellatly of Edinburgh. The mail coach conveyed inside and outside passengers over an uncompleted section of the railway.

'insides' and the 'outsides' – usually four of each. Outside seats were cheaper, but travel by either class was expensive and only the wealthier traveller could afford it. Poorer people either had to make do with a stage wagon or, as most did, walk, but many seldom travelled at all.

The stagecoach passenger had to book at least a day in advance to secure a place in the coach, giving his or her personal details to a clerk in the booking room at the inn. At the start of their journey passengers received a handwritten docket, which served to identify them to the driver or guard, and this document was probably the earliest British transport ticket. The guard held a waybill listing the names of the passengers in his charge; a copy of the docket or the stub from which the ticket was torn remained with the clerk at the coaching inn, who recorded the transaction in a ledger. The driver took

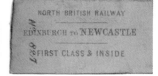

The front of a
Bolton & Leigh
Railway ticket,
and a similar ticket
from the Northern
& Eastern Railway.
Each passenger's
ticket was torn
from a sheet; the
stub was retained
as the waybill.

payment at stages along the route or at the conclusion of the journey.

The railways brought an altogether more comfortable and safer means of transport, although many stagecoach practices remained, especially the method of issuing travel documents. The pioneer railways had evolved from earlier horse-worked wagonways and tramroads, which used open wagons for the transportation of minerals and other goods, coupled up to form a train. Horse traction soon gave way to steam locomotives, and railway technology evolved through the pioneer work of Richard Trevithick, George and Robert Stephenson, and others. Within a few years, several ambitious railway schemes were presented before Parliament. One of the earliest was the Stockton & Darlington Railway (SDR), incorporated on 19 April 1821. At first, railways carried few passengers, and those who travelled had to make do with open trucks designed for the transport of goods, but gradually carriages with bodywork resembling that of stagecoaches were used – not surprisingly, since the artisans who built road coaches supplied many for the railways. An early railway that catered for passengers from the outset was the Liverpool & Manchester Railway (L&MR), authorised on 5 May 1826 and opened on 15 September 1830, following the so-called Rainhill Trials, when the Stephensons' *Rocket* was selected as the most efficient means of traction for the railway, becoming the archetypal design for all steam railway locomotives.

Above: *Rocket* commemorated (by a later replica) on an LNWR postcard.

Liverpool or Manchester to

ROCKET 150

Rainhill and return

Sunday 25 May 1980

Left and below: combined entry tickets to the 150th anniversary celebrations of the Rainhill Trials.

Sunday 25 May 1980   Price £7·50

ROCKET 150

Admission Ticket

STAND   BLOCK   ROW   SEAT
BB   1   A   2

The railways rapidly developed into a system of trunk lines closely following existing transport routes, and soon surpassed the canals, the stagecoach and other road transport for the movement of goods, minerals, livestock, produce and passengers. While the railways revolutionised transport, they retained the old method of issuing handwritten travel documents and waybills adapted from stagecoach practice, but this proved unsuitable for large numbers of passengers. The adoption of Thomas Edmondson's ticketing system solved this administrative problem, revolutionised the entire booking process, and left an internationally recognised and lasting legacy named after its inventor – the Edmondson ticket. Edmondson's name soon became synonymous with the railway ticket, lightheartedly referred to as 'Edmondson's calling card'.

Every proposal for a new railway had to go before Parliament, as had those for canals and turnpikes before them. The parliamentary contest took into account a variety of opposing interests: the railway promoters had to overcome the opposition of landowners and competing railways; the canal and stagecoach companies resisted new railway schemes. Despite vehement opposition, many railways were authorised and built, culminating in a spate of speculative ventures to build over 9,000 miles of railway during the mid-1840s, a period known as the Railway Mania. Throughout this period, advances in railway technology and the growth of the infrastructure prompted passenger numbers to rise steadily and, as Parliament approved more railways, the revenue from passenger tickets rose accordingly.

The British railway ticket – although ephemeral – stood as a record of every journey ever taken on the railways of England, Scotland, Wales and Ireland (the Act of Union 1800 led to the government of Ireland from Westminster, and all Irish railways up to Partition in 1921 became the concern of the United Kingdom Parliament). The ticket – both paper and Edmondson card – serves as the contract between the passenger and the

Elaborate company monograms sometimes appeared on the backs of early British railway tickets: the Edinburgh & Glasgow (EGR), Maryport & Carlisle (MCR) and London & North Western (LNWR). The front of each ticket is shown below the monogram.

Hadlow Road station on the former Hooton to West Kirby line in the Wirral still stands, and retains its booking office, but it closed to passengers in 1956. The ticket is a tangible relic of a lost railway.

railway company and provides evidence of the passenger's entitlement. It also serves as a receipt for fares charged and permits entry to designated areas of railway-owned property, and it accounts for monetary transactions between passenger, railway servant and the railway company. British railway tickets are tangible relics of lost stations and add to the nostalgia of the railways. They also provide a source of interest to social historians, railway enthusiasts and collectors, without whom these remarkable records of forgotten journeys would have been lost forever.

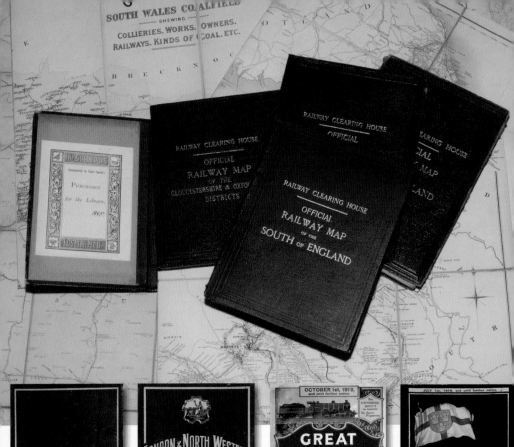

SOUTH WALES CO. ALFIELD
SHEWING
COLLIERIES. WORKS. OWNERS.
RAILWAYS. KINDS OF COAL. ETC.

RAILWAY CLEARING HOUSE
OFFICIAL
RAILWAY MAP
OF THE
GLOUCESTERSHIRE & OXFORD
DISTRICTS

RAILWAY CLEARING HOUSE
OFFICIAL

RAILWAY CLEARING HOUSE
OFFICIAL
RAILWAY MAP
OF THE
SOUTH OF ENGLAND

RAILWAY CLEARING HOUSE

Purchased
for the Library
1895

MIDLAND
TIME TABLES

OCTOBER 1913, TO JUNE 30TH 1914.

LONDON & NORTH WESTERN
RAILWAY
TIME TABLES

OCTOBER 3rd, 1921, and until further notice.

OCTOBER 1st, 1912,
and until further notice.

GREAT
CENTRAL
RAILWAY
TIME TABLES

RAPID
TRAVEL
IN
LUXURY

JULY 1st, 1919, and until further notice.

GREAT EASTERN
RAILWAY
Time Tables.

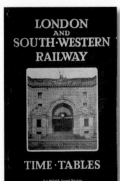

LONDON
AND
SOUTH·WESTERN
RAILWAY

TIME·TABLES

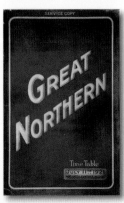

SERVICE COPY

GREAT
NORTHERN

Time Table
JULY 11th 1921

TIME TABLES
LONDON & NORTH WESTERN
RAILWAYS IN CONNECTION

LANCASHIRE YORKSHIRE
&
RAILWAY
TIME TABLES
JULY 1st, 1898, and until further notice

Through Express Services

HEAD OFFICES HUNTS BANK MANCHESTER

THE EDMONDSON TICKET AND RAILWAY TRAVEL IN BRITAIN

Opposite: Railway Clearing House maps were essential documents for apportioning revenue from through routes between railway companies. Timetables were equally important, informing company employees and railway travellers of scheduled services.

THE CONSTANT CLAMOUR for new company flotations and a spate of associated mergers and amalgamations promoted the expansion of a national railway network and increased revenue and profits for the largest emerging railway companies. Smaller companies entered into agreements with nearby larger companies to operate their lines and supply rolling stock, locomotives and labour, which led inexorably to the takeover of the smaller concern by the larger railway. The larger companies, often in direct competition with each other, promoted and built rival routes of their own or entered into mutually beneficial agreements with their competitors to allow through traffic of each other's wagons, carriages and passengers. This interdependency of companies, often brokered by parliamentary intervention, led to complex agreements for apportioning shares of the takings.

Each station had to submit an accurate account of passengers and goods, for its own company and for agreed traffic from adjoining companies. Prearranged local and inter-company working agreements apportioned payments, on a mile and chain basis for goods and passengers, which were determined from waybills, receipts and tickets. All railway companies were also obliged to make statutory returns to the Board of Trade for traffic, and here the station clerk's handwritten travel documents, receipts and waybills were compiled to prepare the company accounts.

Above right: A metal ticket tally issued to third-class passengers at Leicester on the Leicester & Swannington Railway (L&S). They were collected from destination stations by the guard and returned to Leicester for reuse.

Centre right: The London & Greenwich Railway issued metal ticket tallies to operate a turnstile to gain access to the platform and train.

Bottom right:
Metal railway tickets survived for many years on Dinorwic quarry workmen's trains; they were issued to quarrymen for travel to and from their place of work for the duration of their working lives.

Below:
A complimentary
ticket issued to an
employee of the
Railway Clearing
House.

Bottom:
The boardroom
of the Railway
Clearing House.

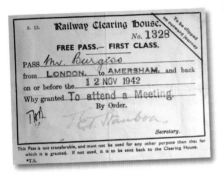

The Edmondson ticketing system after 1838 became an efficient means of administering fares and ensuring their payment. It also allowed efficient accountancy and record-keeping for all passenger traffic, including proportions of fares due from other railways for through services. The railway companies continued to collect and account for revenue from their own tickets, and those of neighbouring companies, but increasingly the Railway Clearing House (RCH) and the Irish Railway Clearing House became responsible for apportioning payment to participating companies.

The RCH held annual conferences for participating companies, which set objectives for through booking of passengers (and carriages) and dividing of receipts on a mileage basis from detailed maps. The RCH advised that their member companies should use Edmondson's patented ticket-printing and date-stamping system, which prompted the widespread adoption of the Edmondson ticket, although by then the Edmondson ticket had already been accepted by many companies.

Thomas Edmondson was born on 30 June 1792 and worked for Gillow, the famous furniture

A ticket cabinet
illustrated in John
B. Edmondson's
catalogue, c. 1905.

manufacturer in Lancaster, having served an apprenticeship as a cabinet-maker. In July 1836, when he was forty-four years old, he took a position as the stationmaster and booking clerk at Milton station on the newly built Newcastle & Carlisle Railway (NCR). (The station was renamed Brampton Junction in 1870 by the North Eastern Railway, which absorbed the line in July 1862.) During the course of his duties at Milton, Edmondson realised that there was no adequate method for checking fares from passengers at wayside stations such as his own, which relied on collecting fares from passengers and then handing the total receipts to the guard of the train. Edmondson was also aware that the method of issuing handwritten travel dockets from major stations was inefficient, and systematic checks of receipts from passengers travelling on the line were inadequate. This prompted him to adopt the simple idea of writing the names of the issuing and collecting stations, a sequential number and the fare on a small piece of card to give to the passenger on payment of the fare. Adding the total fares on all the tickets issued during the day gave an accurate and foolproof tally of the money taken at the station, and the sequential number written on the ticket showed that all tickets were accounted for or if any were missing.

Ticket tubes
dispense tickets
in a numbered
sequence – the
lowest number
first. Chalked on
the slate below
each tube is the
number of the last
ticket sold from
that tube.

Inside Bridgnorth
booking office on
the Severn Valley
Railway.

The action of
inserting a ticket
into the jaw of the
dating press causes
the stamp to strike
the ticket through
the inked ribbon,
leaving an
impression of
the day, month
and year.

Edmondson progressed to a simple inked stamp for printing the tickets,
and a series of tubes to hold the pre-printed tickets for destination stations
and classes of fare in a numbered sequence (the lowest number at the
bottom); the tickets dropped by gravity as the bottom ticket was withdrawn.

He made the dating press himelf, using his carpentry
skills, after getting the idea from a hinged pocket comb,
the sharp motion of pushing a card towards the hinge
effectively closing and nipping the card. The wooden
press used an inked ribbon and changeable date
numbers and letter dies; the design was the prototype
for all future dating presses. The number sequence of
tickets in each tube started at zero, which meant that
at the end of each day the number of the next ticket
remaining in the tube represented the total number
sold. A running total was chalked on to an inlaid piece
of slate in front of the tube and the number was
recorded in a ledger. Multiplied by the fare, this
running total subtracted from the previous day's figure
would give the daily takings for that particular tube for
that day. Another component of the system was the
ticket-printing machine, which was able to print
thousands of tickets in sequentially numbered batches.
The press was later improved by James Carson,
foreman at the Edmondson works.

In 1839 Edmondson took the post of chief booking clerk at Manchester on the Manchester & Leeds Railway (MLR), where he was allowed to develop his system; he left in 1841 to develop and market his ideas commercially. Edmondson supplied many of the early British railways with facilities and services licensed under the terms of his patent. The licence royalty was £15 for railways not exceeding 30 miles in length and £20 for 40 miles etc, later fixed at a rate of 10 shillings per mile. After Thomas Edmondson's death on 22 June 1851 the John B. Edmondson Railway Ticket and Apparatus Company, of Knowsley Street, Cheetham, Manchester, owned by his son, continued to supply tickets to the railways. Edmondson did, however, have competition: Waterlow & Sons was a significant rival for the manufacture of ticket printing and dating equipment, increasingly expanding their Edmondson ticket business after Edmondson's patents expired.

Edmondson had revolutionised the entire fare-collection process and introduced a patent pasteboard ticket size of 2 ¼ by 1 ¼ inches, with printed details, and multiple colours and designs. His system proved to be the best and most efficient way of collecting revenue from the ever-increasing numbers of travellers on the expanding railway system throughout Britain. Improved upon by his company and its rivals over the years, the system saw

Above left: A pre-1900 Waterlow & Sons Edmondson ticket-printing press from the former BR printing centre at Crewe, now used by the preserved Severn Valley Railway to print tickets.

Top right: Dies used in the Waterlow & Sons press.

Below right: Rotary number wheels fitted in the press, with the ticket slide and bridge removed.

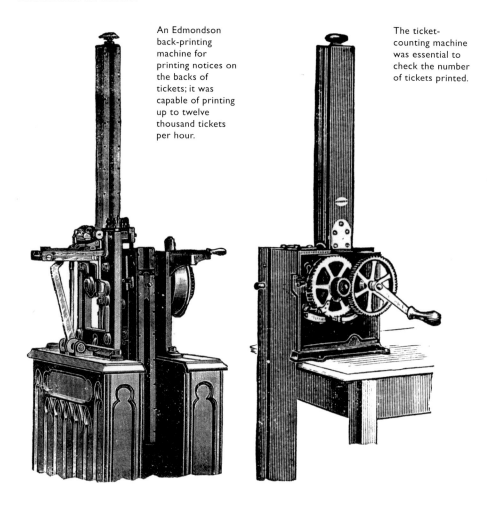

An Edmondson back-printing machine for printing notices on the backs of tickets; it was capable of printing up to twelve thousand tickets per hour.

The ticket-counting machine was essential to check the number of tickets printed.

service on British Railways (BR) until finally replaced by the Accountancy Passenger Ticket Issuing System (APTIS) and the portable version, PORTIS, in the late 1980s. The Waterlow & Sons presses at the BR paper and printing centre in Crewe finally ended their printing runs in 1988. However, a number of presses found their way to preserved railways and continue to print Edmondson tickets.

Mills Hill station on the Manchester & Leeds Railway closed on 11 August 1842, three years after that section of line opened. Remarkably, a few tickets survived and are preserved.

Different colours of Edmondson tickets appeared over time, in corporate colours or to aid identification by railway servants. There was no universally adopted colour or pattern, and companies had their own colour schemes to identify categories of tickets or class of passenger; in some instances, different colours represented the direction of travel on a line. Company monograms also appeared on the backs of some early Edmondson tickets to identify the issuing company to auditors at the RCH. Blank Edmondson tickets without preprinted destination or issuing station names were also used, partly because it was never possible to hold a complete selection of preprinted tickets for every possible destination – a shortcoming of the Edmondson ticket system. From the early 1840s onwards, the Edmondson ticketing procedure had become a familiar and well-rehearsed process for all railway servants and travellers. It started with the passenger stating his or her destination and paying a fare at the hatch in the booking hall; machine-issued tickets appeared much later. One of the earliest mechanised ticket-issuing machines, a German-manufactured Ragina printing machine, was installed at Snow Hill station in Birmingham in 1911. The passenger needed to keep the issued ticket on his or her person for the duration of the journey. A dated ticket gave the passenger authority to travel, identified the destination, and informed railway staff of restrictions of travel, class and entitlements. Inevitably, passengers had to present their tickets to claim these rights. The first inspection

A machine that once issued GWR platform tickets, preserved at Highley station on the SVR, and an example of such a ticket.

Below:
A ticket from a Ragina automated ticket-issuing machine installed at Birmingham Snow Hill station in 1911.

A selection of free issue and priced platform tickets. Ticket 1719 permitted access to an Underground platform during the bombing of London in the Second World War.

RAILWAY TICKET NIPPERS.

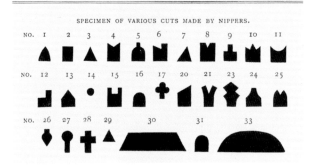

SPECIMEN OF VARIOUS CUTS MADE BY NIPPERS.

The ticket nipper shows that a ticket had passed inspection; from John B. Edmondson's catalogue.

A ticket examiner on the LNWR.

was usually at the barrier on entry to the platform; non-travel platform tickets issued at the booking office or from a vending machine were also scrutinised.

Passengers sometimes had their tickets checked and clipped on their train by a travelling ticket-inspector who patrolled corridor-connected carriages; inspectors also visited trains when they stopped at stations and left the carriages before the train started. The inspector ensured that third-class passengers did not travel first class, and that passengers had actually purchased a ticket and were not trying to evade payment. Single tickets were collected at the destination station; occasionally they were collected at special ticket platforms a mile or so from the destination. Return tickets were halved by tearing, or just clipped on the destination half, and the return portion was handed back to the passenger for the return journey to the issuing station. Collected tickets were taken to the station office, where they were recorded and bagged up in pouches or envelopes, to be sent to the audit department of the railway company, together with station receipts and takings from the booking office. The company office would then account for local and inter-company receipts in accordance with working agreements, and forward tickets to the issuing company or the RCH for audit.

The issuing company would also send copies of their stations' returns and the tickets they collected to their company office, where they were accounted or forwarded to the RCH. At the RCH, the audit procedure entailed laying out groups of whole tickets and halves by ticket type, i.e. ordinary, tourist, season or excursion, on numerous tables; employees then performed the task of compiling passenger returns. The RCH operated two procedures for apportioning payments from ticket sales: the first procedure was by 'two companies group', in which payment was made by the RCH to the receiving company and debited from the issuing company. The second, when the journey traversed more than two companies' tracks, was the 'three companies group', where the RCH received the appropriate portion of the total receipts from the issuing company, the issuing company retaining its portion of the takings from its station. The RCH distributed the balance of the money received proportionally to the non-booking companies along the route and issued appropriate monthly receipts.

A travelling ticket-inspector on the preserved SVR inspects a first-class passenger's ticket.

The RCH was founded at an inaugural meeting at 11 Drummond Street, London NW1, near Euston Square, on 2 January 1842. George Carr Glyn and Kenneth Morison, officers of the London & Birmingham Railway, convened the meeting and invited representatives of other railways. Membership was voluntary and subscription was from annual fees per station and a levy from receipts. Within thirty years, most railway companies had joined. After the Grouping of the Railways Act in 1923, the RCH continued in a new role standardising railway operations. Following nationalisation under the Transport Act of 1947, the organisation finally disbanded on 31 March 1963. During its existence, the RCH handled many millions of issued tickets returned by participating railway companies for audit.

Most Edmondson tickets ended up in the ticket-shredding machine.

Every month the railway companies efficiently disposed of hundreds of thousands of their redundant tickets, using another Edmondson invention, the ticket-shredding machine; very few tickets survived. Inevitably, as the era of steam grew to a close and the popularity of trainspotting reached a peak, the audit department of BR also became a source of used tickets for the railway-ticket collector.

This GWR handbill advertises special tickets for a sheep-shearing event.

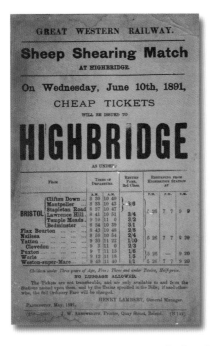

GREAT WESTERN RAILWAY.

Sheep Shearing Match

AT HIGHBRIDGE

On Wednesday, June 10th, 1891,

CHEAP TICKETS

WILL BE ISSUED TO

HIGHBRIDGE

AS UNDER

Travel on the railways was heavily advertised and promoted; each company issued its own comprehensive timetables and summaries of routes and services, and railway guides such as Bradshaw made the information available to the travelling public. Promotional handbills advertised special fares and excursions and special tickets. Changes to services, routes and lines, and the amalgamation of railway companies, also brought about changes in the appearance of Edmondson tickets, and a period of transition before a new style superseded an older one. The Grouping of British railway companies in 1923 resulted in four railway empires: the Great Western Railway (GWR) (the only major pre-Grouping railway company that survived the amalgamations); the London Midland & Scottish Railway (LMS); the London & North Eastern Railway (LNER); and the Southern Railway (SR) – collectively known as the 'Big Four'. At the time of the Grouping, there were 120 separately owned railways in the British Isles, each with their own stocks of tickets.

The Transport Act of 1947 effectively nationalised the Big Four and created a Railway Executive incorporated into the British Transport

A selection of tickets from some of the larger railway companies that were absorbed by the GWR in 1923.

Left and below: Tickets of some of the main companies that merged to form the LMS, including 9965 North London Railway (NLR), 686 North Staffordshire Railway (NSR), and 4718 Glasgow & South Western Railway (GSWR).

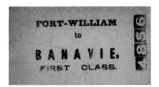

Above: This LMS handbill advertises ticket deals for a popular whippet race meeting at Penrith.

Left and below: Tickets of pre-Grouping railways that came together to form the LNER, including 4856 North British Railway (NBR), 5176 Great Northern Railway (GNR), 3340 Great Central Railway (GCR), 770 North Eastern Railway (NER), and 387 Hull & Barnsley Railway (HBR).

21

Left: Cheap day tickets advertised on a Southern Railway handbill.

Above: Tickets from the four main Pre-Grouping railways that constituted the Southern Railway: 4289 is from the joint management committee set up in 1899 to manage the affairs of the South Eastern Railway (SER) and the London, Chatham & Dover (LCDR).

Tickets from British Railways regions, and post-dated LNER ticket from Pool-in-Wharfedale sent to a collector ten days before the station closed on 22 March 1965.

Commission (BTC) on 1 January 1948. The BTC was divided into six operational regions: Southern, Eastern, North Eastern, London Midland, Western, and Scottish. Nationalisation of the railways also brought with it a measure of standardisation for railway tickets, although each region retained some individuality, and transitional types appeared for a time. The BTC was abolished after fifteen years and replaced by the British Railways Board (BRB) under the 1962 Transport Act; its newly appointed chairman was Dr Richard Beeching. During the 1960s, it was possible to purchase old stock pre-nationalisation tickets from BR stations – some scheduled for closure under the Beeching plan – and many postdated GWR, LMS, LNER and SR tickets were issued to collectors.

Another group of railways remained wholly independent and did not amalgamate or join the Grouping, and some remained independent even after nationalisation. Other companies operated as joint lines and joint committees, formed between rival railway interests at a point of contact between them. These joint lines had their own boards and were nominally independent of the parent companies. Independent companies and joint lines issued their own tickets. Alternatively, joint lines issued tickets belonging to their parent company valid over the joint line. Sometimes it was possible to buy a ticket from a joint station for either constituent company's train or carriage over a joint line, or over other companies' rails where running rights existed.

A selection of tickets from joint line committees.

THE GRAND JUNCTION RAILWAY

Winsford is a typical British station, on the Grand Junction Railway (GJR). Both station and railway opened to passengers on the same day, 4 July 1837. The GJR was conceived as part of an ambitious scheme to link Manchester, Liverpool and Birmingham to London, by joining the Warrington & Newton Railway (WNR), which already connected to the Liverpool & Manchester Railway. The scheme proved successful and was adequately financed, and engineered by George Stephenson, Joseph Locke and John Rastrick. Within ten years, the GJR had consolidated with other companies and on 16 July 1846 became a constituent part of the London & North Western Railway (LNWR). In 1923 it was grouped into the LMS and at nationalisation in 1948 came under BR London Midland Region, firstly under BTC control and then under the BRB. London Midland now operates the station, which is served by trains between Birmingham New Street and Liverpool Lime Street.

Winsford station as it appeared in BR days before electrification, with internal and external views of its ticket ofice, and some tickets sold there. Tickets were issued under LNWR ownership, then after 1923 under LMS control, and finally under British Railways.

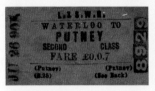

TYPES OF TICKET

THERE ARE MANY different types of British railway travel ticket, but they all fall into three distinct categories. The first represents a 'single' journey: a ticket issued from one station to a destination station. Railway companies soon decided to issue fares at reduced rates for two-way journeys, which became the second category: a 'return' ticket. The third category was the 'excursion' ticket, which offered reduced fares at specified times over certain routes, at the discretion of the railway – for example, to the races or a football match, or to seaside or spa resorts, often on a bank holiday or a Saturday. Thomas Cook's first temperance excursion was on 5 July 1841 on the Midland Counties Railway. British railway companies also offered different fare scales to different categories of passenger – first, second, third or even fourth class. Facilities for third-class passengers were minimal. Parliament was concerned about how the railways operated passenger services and passed legislation to promote safe transport for third-class passengers, following an accident on the GWR near Reading in the winter of 1841, when several third-class passengers were killed by being thrown out of an open carriage in a derailment. In 1844 the President of the Board of Trade, W. E. Gladstone, introduced an Act to compel railway companies to run at least one passenger train with seats protected from the weather each way daily, at no less than 12 mph. The Act introduced the 'parliamentary fare' at a 'parl'y' or 'government rate' of no more than 1d per mile. The same Act also introduced half-price 'child' fares for children between three and twelve years old (younger children travelled free).

The 1889 Regulation of Railways Act required companies to display fares for all journeys, and changes in legislation and fares resulted in different information appearing on tickets. Contract tickets soon appeared, better known as season tickets, issued to daily travellers for multiple journeys, usually to and from a place of work. The railway companies also issued 'privilege' tickets to their employees and their families at a quarter-rate reduced fare, and also identified different categories of passenger on tickets, such as workpeople, fisher people, soldiers, sailors and airmen on duty or on leave, and shipwrecked mariners.

The London Necropolis railway offered a choice of first-, second- and third-class tickets for its deceased passengers travelling in a coffin.

Opposite: Details on LSWR Edmondson tickets changed over time. Fares, the full title of the company and miniature repeats appeared in the 1890s. After 1890 serial numbers appeared on the left-hand side, and the wording of conditions changed after 1914.

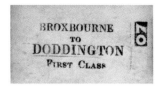  

The information on the earliest British railway tickets was often limited to the sequential number, issuing and destination stations, and class of passenger. Parliamentary fare passengers often had to make do with open carriages, sometimes without seats.

The sequentially numbered ticket identified the journey and the class and category of passenger, but sometimes omitted other details – even the company name. The railway companies also advertised and sold tickets in bulk or at preferential rates to companies, institutions, clubs and societies. They also promoted reduced fares during the summer for holiday travel and excursions. Many specially printed tickets were available for other railway-owned transport services, including coastal steamers, ferries, river boats, buses and even aircraft. As well as travel tickets for passengers, there were many different types of 'article' tickets, and tickets for the transport of animals – mainly dogs, cats and hunting horses. Article tickets identified bicycles, tricycles, carts, musical instruments and various forms of baggage and produce.

Further categories of Edmondson card tickets, not defined strictly in terms of type, but with identifying characteristics and features of interest, include:

Issued tickets, usually clipped and dated, representing a true journey.

Unissued specimen, with no clips or date stamp, sometimes stamped with 'specimen' or 'cancelled', and never used for a journey. BR (Southern) audit tickets are stamped on the back '1955'.

Unissued double clipped (unused) with no date stamp, but with two uniformly spaced audit office clips either side of the ticket.

Transitional: a ticket similar in appearance to an earlier type, especially after the transfer of ownership of a company. Tickets often appeared in the old company style with the new company name.

Spuriously dated or clipped by collectors as keepsakes, sometimes issued with inappropriate lettering and dates, or clipped with the wrong style of nipper, outwardly appearing as a genuine journey. They are rare, but see Bishop's Castle Railway (BCR) on page 44.

Handwritten blank Edmondsons stamped, dated and representing a true journey, but occasionally some are spurious.

Mechanised tickets: machine-issued card tickets, e.g. Multiprinter, Flexiprinter, National Cash Register NCR21 and NCR24.

Non-Edmondson tickets include the following categories:
Paper tickets: there are many different examples, including travel warrants – handwritten or typed, usually on single sheets of paper of varying sizes.
Bell Punch types supplied by a conductor on the train from a hand-held rack, with destinations sometimes in the form of a ladder, or geographically numbered or named stages. The action of punching a hole in the ticket against the fare stage rang a bell on the punching machine.
Mechanised paper-ribbon machine-issued tickets printed at the point of purchase: Handiprinter, Omniprinter, Ultimate and Ultimatic are common examples.
PORTIS (Portable Ticket Issuing System), **APTIS** (Accountancy Passenger Ticket Issuing System, sometimes called All Purpose Ticket Issuing System), **SPOTIS** (Simplified Operated Ticket Issuing System), all credit-card size.
Railcards: modern flat-rate tickets.

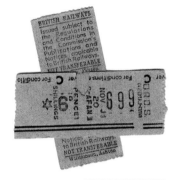

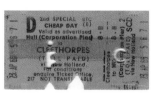

Some examples of mechanised tickets: 699 Setright Speed, 24998 and 02892 Ultimatic, 1 49854 Ultimate, 5671 Flexiprinter, and 1911 NCR21.

Left: APTIS and PORTIS tickets.

The table shows a further selection of specially printed categories of Edmondson ticket offered by many British railway companies, although the list by no means covers every type that was available:

RAILWAY SERVICES

ADMISSIONS
Air-raid shelter LPTB platform
Exams (LMS)
Railway and event/admission
Zoological gardens, etc

ANIMAL
Dog or cat
Hunting horse

ARTICLE
Bicycle
Canoe
Mail cart, go-cart, perambulator
Musical instrument
Pedal ice-cream tricycle (LMS)
Sawing machine

COMBINED MODES OF TRAVEL
Permit
Rail motor car
River and rail

COMMEMORATIVE
100 years anniversary railway
Commemorative
Commemorative (event)
Souvenir

EXCHANGE TICKETS
Journey
Class
To or from bus

MEALS
Dinner

Luncheon
Packed lunch
Tea

RAILWAY-OWNED SERVICES
Ferry
Hotel ticket
Facility ticket

SERVICES
Bicycle (storage)
Cloakroom
Parking
Reserved seat or compartment
Tricycle

SPECIAL PASSENGER CATEGORIES

CIVIL DEFENCE PERSONNEL
Civil Defence bomb disposal worker
Civil Defence
Militia
Police
Territorial Force
Volunteer

ENTERTAINERS
Band, orchestral company
Choir
Circus
Concert party
Dramatic society
Music-hall artiste
Pantomime company
Theatrical company

GOVERNMENT EMPLOYEES
Customs officer
Government training centre
Juvenile camp attendant
Ministry of Labour

MARITIME PERSONNEL
Shipwrecked mariner
Ship's crew
Mercantile Marine on leave
Training-ship boy

SCHOLARS
Schools specials

Sunday school party

SERVICE PERSONNEL
Cadet
HM forces on leave/duty
Military on duty
Military on leave (furlough)
Munitions worker
Naval boy on leave
Naval visit
Navy, Army or Air Force officer
Soldier/sailor on duty/leave
Yeomanry

CARERS AND PATIENTS
Ambulance
Asylum
Blind person and attendant
Convalescent home
Orphan
Poor child on holiday
Poor child's attendant
Relative visiting evacuees
Coffin ticket (London Necropolis)

SPORTS PEOPLE
Angler
Bather
Boy Scout
County rifle club
Curler
Excursion rugby

Excursion sporting event
Football
Golfer/golf caddie
Motor racing
Racecourse
Rural ramble
Social and athletic association
Speedway racing
Sports club

WORK PEOPLE
Apprentice
Cattleman
Colliery workman
Commercial traveller
Drover
Fish worker/fisher people
Forestry or farming camp
Groom horses (LMS)
Harvestman
Hop picker
Kent mine worker
Mill girl
Quarry worker
Trainer
Workman (general)
Workman (late)
Workman (middle shift)
Workman (night)
Market ticket
Market/market free

SPECIAL FARES

EXCURSIONS
Bargain travel
Evening cheap
Excursion (various)
Holiday
Special trip
Summer ticket
Tourist
Tour
Weekend

PARTY BOOKINGS
Conference
Charter control
Company party
Continental party
Party
Picnic pleasure party
Pleasure party
Society
Walking tour

Bulk travel

PRIVILEGE FARES
Foreign
Local
Colonial
Interchange
Company employee
Preservation society member
Director
Complimentary
Railway employee
Shareholder
Voter

STATUTORY FARES
Government approved rates
Child (occasionally juvenile)

SPECIAL TRAINS
'Bournemouth Belle'

'Brighton Belle'
'Devon Belle'
'Golden Arrow'
'Kentish Belle'
Pullman
Pullman carriage
'Silver Jubilee'
'Southern Belle'
'Thanet Belle'
'The Coronation'
'West Riding Limited'
Sleeping carriage
Passenger by foods train

TRANSFER FARES
Trans-Britain
Emigrant
Trans-migrant
Ocean cruise passenger
Ocean passenger

The Edmondson ticket usually appeared with horizontal print, that is in landscape format, and less frequently in vertical or portrait format; sometimes the fronts of tickets were printed vertically and the backs horizontally. Return tickets had perforations to permit them to be torn in half or into thirds. Severed half-tickets found in most collections are either the outbound or the homebound portions of a return; some tour tickets had three portions, combining travel by river, road and rail. There were also halved singles issued as child-rate tickets; miniature repeats printed on both sides of the ticket preserved essential information in each half. Additional information also appeared on certain categories of ticket and included details about special trains, combination with other modes of transport such as buses or ships, and date and time of use. The company name in full or abbreviated, the class of passenger, and the issuing station name (in smaller letters) and destination station name in bolder type, reversed in the two halves of a return ticket, were also printed. Some tickets also show issuing numbers for stations and automated issuing points, agency numbers, issuing point codes and permitted routes.

Symbols and geometric shapes also appeared on tickets in the form of triangles, ovals, squares and circles – in solid colours or as printed outlines. They normally identified platform tickets, but some squares and circles on transport tickets symbolised inner and outer circle routes as on the London Underground. Sometimes overprinted numbers represented destination stations and appeared on commuter tickets; the table on page 33 shows some of the letters and numbers overprinted in large type on the face of Edmondson tickets to aid identification (the list is not comprehensive).

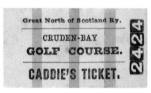

A selection of tickets from the table on pages 30 and 31, from 'Animal' to 'Article', 'Fisher People' to 'Shipwrecked Mariners', and 'Voters' travelling to their constituencies.

OVERPRINTS

Above: A platform ticket permitted a visitor timed access to meet or wave off passengers. In the final years of steam on British railways, trainspotters and railway enthusiasts inevitably purchased a platform ticket to witness the scene from the platform edge.

1	Return excursion day trip	L	Long period
1/2D	Half-day trip	L	Leave
1D	One-day trip	M	Market
AC	Athletic club	M	Monthly
B	Bus journey	MD	Mid-day return
C	Cheap ticket	MW	Mid-week
CD	Cheap day	O	Outer (London Underground)
CH	Convalescent home	PR	Privilege
Child	Child's fare (017, page 32)	R	Return (0886, page 32)
D	Day ticket	RR	River and rail
D	Dog	S	Summer ticket
DR	Day return	S	Steamer journey
FH	Fruit and hop picker	SF	Single fare
FM	Friday to Monday	SL	Service leave
FM	Folding mailcart	SM	Saturday to Monday
GR	Government rate	ST	Special trip
I	Inner Circle (London Underground)	WE	Weekend
		WT	Walking tour

Advertisements sometimes appeared on Edmondson tickets – some LMS tickets had a pull-out advertisement tab – but more often conditions were printed on the backs.

Examples of vertical tickets from the Midland, Southern, London & South Western, London Brighton & South Coast and North Eastern railways.

Many Edmondson tickets were printed with different-coloured stripes or bands, and on different designs of card, to make them more difficult to counterfeit, and to help identify them to railway staff.

Some GWR and LNER blank tickets had a security background – an intricate pattern that changed when written on; subsequent erasure or alteration could then be seen in the pattern. Tickets also had printed statements either on the front or on the back saying 'Issued subject to byelaws, company regulations and to the conditions in company bills, notices and timetables', and sometimes 'This ticket is not transferable'. Very occasionally, a series of Edmondson tickets would have printed advertisements on their backs, but this was uncommon and the practice was mainly restricted to tram and bus tickets. The LMS did, however, issue tickets with advertisements on pull-out tags.

Railways opened under the Light Railways Act 1896 invariably used the same types and categories of ticket as conventional railways. The Act applied to lightly engineered standard-gauge lines, narrow-gauge railways and local corporation street tramways, the distinction between a tramway and a light railway being no more than that a tramway usually runs on streets and railways usually do not, although many tramways purported to be railways and vice versa. Tramway tickets were normally issued by a travelling conductor at fare stages, and dispensed from a ticket rack or Bell Punch. Bell Punch tickets had a ladder of stations or stops printed on their face laid out in geographical order, sometimes written out in full or shown as numbered fare stages. A single ladder was used for a single-fare ticket; a divided ladder symbolised different directions of travel such as up and down or inner and outer routes. Each fare stage appeared printed on each side of the ladder, although in a different order. A separately priced ticket was used for each fare, representing the distance and number of stops travelled. The direction of travel was indicated by whichever part of the ladder showed the punched hole, and on divided-ladder tickets the furthest extent of travel was indicated on the fare stage opposite the punched hole.

Some railways adopted a similar ticketing practice, especially on rural routes and rail-bus services.

Companies used every opportunity to promote their routes and advertised special tickets to various groups of passengers. The commuter category took advantage of reduced-fare season tickets, offered by companies to promote travel between suburbs and city centres. The season or contract ticket, sometimes called a 'free ticket' (for travelling freely, rather than free of charge), offered unlimited travel between two stations. In inner London, the trunk lines were linked by a series of connecting lines: the West London (WLR) and West London Extension Railways (WLER) formed a connection between the GWR, LNWR, London & South Western (LSWR) and London Brighton & South Coast (LBSCR). Similarly, the North London Railway (NLR) offered an intensive commuter service that served to link the LNWR, GWR, Midland, Great Northern (GNR), London Tilbury & Southend (LTSR) and Great Eastern Railway (GER).

A selection of Bell Punch tickets from the Southern Railway rail motor service, the Welsh Highland Railway, the Cleobury Mortimer & Ditton Priors Railway (CMDPR), the GWR Chalford line, and BR local services from London Paddington.

Kensington Olympia station on the West London and West London Extension Railway (WLR and WLER) in the 1960s, and a ticket from the line.

The Metropolitan Railway also operated a number of commuter services from Baker Street to the edge of the Chiltern Hills, and its subsidiary company Metropolitan Country Estates, formed in 1919, offered affordable modern housing on large estates served by the railway, promoting the housing developments as 'Metro-Land'. Regular trains from the city served

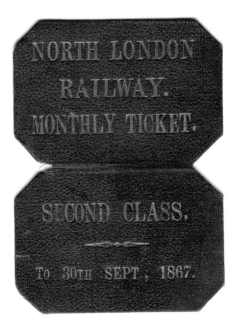

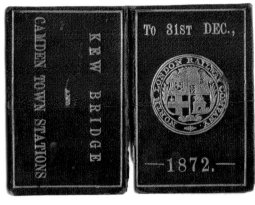

North London Railway season passes.

the estates at Willesden, Wembley, Harrow and Ruislip. The Metropolitan &
Great Central (MGCR) joint line served Chorleywood and the Weller Estate
at Amersham. Other regional cities operated suburban railway networks on
a similar pattern to London, most notably Birmingham, Nottingham,
Manchester and Liverpool, where commuter lines continue to serve the
Wirral and Southport.

The London Passenger Transport Board (LPTB), formed in 1933, and
colloquially known as the 'London Underground', offered another form of
urban railway transport service. The Underground had evolved from
individual companies that merged to form an integrated network of railways
serving the inner-city areas of London, its railway termini and the commuter
belt. The merger of the Baker Street & Waterloo, City & South London,
Hampstead, Piccadilly, London Electric Railway and Metropolitan District
formed Underground Electric Railways (UER). The LPTB formed when the
UER joined with the Central London, Great Northern & City, Hammersmith
& City, Metropolitan and the Metropolitan & GWR Joint. Other lines were
absorbed after the formation of the London Transport Executive (LTE) in
1948. London Transport tickets are unique in their own right, issued by the
constituent companies over their individual routes; Edmondson tickets,
platform tickets and automated-issue tickets offer a wide scope for the
railway-ticket collector.

Another electrically operated mass-transit railway, the Liverpool
Overhead Railway (LOR), opened in stages between 1893 and 1896. It was

 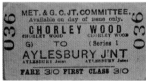 

Commuters' tickets from the
Metropolitan & Great Central
(MGCR) joint line.

37

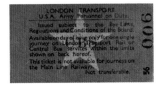

Above:
A selection
of London
Underground
tickets.

affectionately nicknamed the 'Dockers' Umbrella' because it ran on elevated tracks above the streets and the Dock Road and provided shelter for dock workers, ships' crews and passengers in the port of Liverpool. The line closed in December 1956, but tickets survive.

Railways promoted tourist and excursion tickets for additional summer services during holiday months and helped develop tourism and travel for pleasure by offering generous discounts on tickets and allowing breaks in journeys. Companies were keen to promote travel for pleasure and published tourist guides, maps and promotional literature, extolling the countryside and its attractions. Some picturesque rural lines relied heavily on this holiday traffic, especially narrow-gauge railways in Wales, and those serving the picturesque coastal resorts of Devon and Cornwall.

A handbill
advertising fares
on the Liverpool
Overhead Railway
(LOR).

Above and left: An LOR electric train approaches Herculaneum station from Dingle, and four LOR issued tickets; overprinted red numbers symbolised stations on the line.

Three rows above: Tickets from narrow-gauge tourist lines.

HOW TICKETS TELL THE
STORY OF A RAILWAY

A RAILWAY TICKET may hold a great deal of information about travel in former times, either on a line still in existence or for a journey on an abandoned railway. Here a selection of tickets from various specialised collections is used to illustrate a particular route or journey, and at the same time to show how the information printed on them can shed light on the social history of the line and the railway company that issued them. The routes and journeys chosen comprise main lines, branch lines and interesting independent railways, some of which survive to the present day, while others are now long closed and largely forgotten. The railways of Britain are varied and diverse; each has its own unique character. All serve different aims and objectives for the traveller.

The Severn Valley Railway (SVR) is a typical example of what was a busy GWR branch line. 16 miles of the former 39 ½-mile route have survived as one of Britain's best-loved heritage steam railways. Services run throughout the year through Worcestershire and Shropshire alongside the River Severn between Bridgnorth, Bewdley and the southern terminus of the line at Kidderminster. The tickets from former companies that owned the line (up to and including today's Severn Valley Railway [Holdings] plc) tell its story. The earliest period of the railway's history is from 1862, when the line was opened as a route between Worcester and Shrewsbury. The West Midland Railway worked the SVR, which branched off from the GWR's Oxford Worcester & Wolverhampton (OWWR) line at Hartlebury.

Two junction stations served to link the line with the GWR & LNWR Joint Shrewsbury to Hereford line. The first was at Bewdley, from where the Tenbury & Bewdley line ran through the Wyre Forest and Cleobury

Opposite:
Arley station on the preserved Severn Valley Railway in March 2010. The midday Bridgnorth-bound train awaits the passing train from Highley – the guard checks his watch. The tickets shown were issued from Highley and Arley in GWR days.

From the earliest years of the Severn Valley line, the West Midland Railway issued tickets for the SVR.

Mortimer to Woofferton Junction. The other junction station was Buildwas, connecting through Much Wenlock with the Shrewsbury to Hereford line north of Craven Arms. There was also a link from Buildwas to the GWR's Shrewsbury to Birmingham line via Coalbrookdale. The SVR was consolidated into the GWR in 1872, which in 1878 opened a connection to Kidderminster.

Above and top of opposite page: Tickets between Hartlebury and Shrewsbury (5994 via Bewdley and the Kidderminster loop, now part of the preserved SVR). The Stourport line closed to passengers in 1970 and was lifted from Hartlebury in 1980.

BR closed the line from Shrewsbury to Alveley in 1963 and withdrew passenger services as far as Bewdley; passenger services between Hartlebury, Bewdley and Kidderminster were withdrawn in 1970. The Severn Valley Railway Society was founded in 1965 and operated its first service from Bridgnorth to Hampton Loade in May 1970. Following the closure of Alveley Colliery and the line thence to Bewdley in 1969, and the subsequent withdrawal of BR services to Bewdley and Stourport in 1970, the Society was able to purchase the line as far as Foley Park Halt, from where the line to Kidderminster was still used by the sugar-beet factory. Services to Bewdley commenced in 1974 and Kidderminster was finally reached in 1984. Like many former railways, much of the old SVR route still exists, snaking its way through the countryside on embankments and through cuttings, under and over bridges, and some stations have survived now privately owned, but there are no plans to reinstate any more of the line. A few railway tickets remain as a reminder of former times when the SVR served as a through route from Worcester to Shrewsbury.

Two much less successful independent lines in a sparsely populated part of Shropshire, just a few miles west of the SVR, have a very different history. The Bishop's Castle Railway (BCR) was authorised by an Act of Parliament on 28 June 1861 and was planned to be a 19-mile-long line from Stretford Bridge at Craven Arms on the Shrewsbury and Hereford line to a junction

Bewdley's other lost branch crossed Dowles Bridge and the River Severn and headed through the Wyre Forest. This railway was not preserved but the trackbed can be followed as part of National Cycle Route 45.

with the Oswestry & Newtown Railway (ONR), later part of the Cambrian Railways, near Montgomery, with a branch from Lydham Heath to Bishop's Castle. The BCR was strapped for capital from the outset and only 9 ½ miles of track, from Craven Arms to the terminus at Bishop's Castle, were built; all further expansion of the line was abandoned. The line went into receivership soon after opening to Lydham Heath on 1 February 1866. After lying moribund for over ten years, it reopened on 2 July 1877; never making a profit and constantly in debt, the railway operated under receivership for over sixty-nine years until it finally closed on 21 April 1935.

Certain known souvenir hunters collected unused tickets from station booking offices after a line closed and dated tickets spuriously a year or so before closure.

The BCR was a shoestring operation for all of its life, but the study of its tickets has shed more light on the history of this rural line. The story of the company's meagre income from ticket sales and

The low serial numbers for first-class tickets on the Bishop's Castle Railway show that only a few were ever needed for intermediate stations, whereas higher numbers for second and third class indicate that there was a greater demand for these.

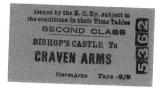

goods revenue is now part of Shropshire folklore, as is a bizarre incident, which came about from yet another financial predicament.

The widow of a BCR director successfully prosecuted the company for non-payment of money owed to her husband for the sale of land. Bailiffs erected a barrier across the line and stopped trains travelling across the disputed land, which effectively isolated Bishop's Castle from the national network. The railway, unable to operate from Craven Arms to its first station at Horderley, conveyed passengers over this section by horse and carriage. Frustrated by the impasse, employees of the BCR enticed the two bailiffs

Here tickets have been marked with revised fares, indicating that they lay in the ticket rack for a long time while the cost of the fare increased.

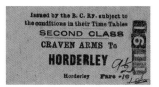

guarding the barrier to a local pub; whilst the bailiffs were temporarily distracted from their duties, a train passed over the section. This action failed to break the deadlock, however, and, to survive, the company settled its outstanding debt, but the reprieve was short-lived as continuing financial problems and competition from buses and commercial road traffic eventually forced the line to close completely.

The second rural Shropshire line was the Potteries, Shrewsbury & North Wales Railway – called the 'Potts' locally. Opened in August 1866 between Shrewsbury Abbey station and Llanymynech on the ONR, with a branch from Kinnerley to Criggion, the company closed in December of the same year because of lack of money. Two years later, it reopened when funds became available, but an official receiver was appointed in 1877, and the line once again succumbed to closure in 1881. An unsuccessful attempt to reopen the line was made around 1888 by the Shropshire Railway Company, but it was only in 1911 that the line reopened again under a Light Railway Order as the Shropshire & Montgomeryshire Light Railway (SMR) in the charge of Colonel Holman F. Stephens. Passenger services ceased in November 1933, eighteen

The Shropshire & Montgomeryshire Railway stretched 18 miles from Shrewsbury Abbey station to Llanymynech, with a 5-mile branch to Criggion from Kinnerley Junction.

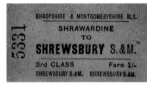

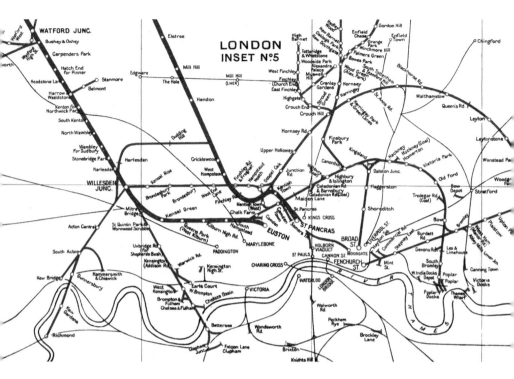

An LMS map showing the company's main lines and London termini.

1930s tickets for the LMS 'Coronation Scot'.

months before the BCR closed. The line received a reprieve after the outbreak of war in 1939, when the army used it to serve local supply depots. It finally closed in 1960. Tickets from the Colonel Stephens era surface from time to time, tangible evidence that this lost line once had a passenger service.

In stark contrast to these poorly funded and failing rural lines, the history of two immensely prestigious and highly successful companies with rival express routes is another example where tickets tell a story. The LMS and LNER main lines from London to the north of England and Scotland followed the west and east coasts respectively, and both companies operated a sprawling network of railways that fed into their respective trunk routes. They were also the two largest companies of the four concerns formed at the Grouping.

The LMS also operated lines in Ireland and claimed to be the largest transport undertaking in Europe.

Both the LMS and the LNER ran efficient publicity departments that exploited every form of printed media from pamphlets and guidebooks to postcards and posters, and their marketing claimed a better, faster, more comfortable or speedier service than their competitors. The rivalry between these companies was fiercest for the lucrative passenger traffic from London to the north and Scotland.

During their twenty-four years of existence, from 1923, through the period of the Second World War, up to nationalisation of the railways at the end of 1947, the companies developed unique and distinct characters. The LMS under Chief Mechanical Engineer (CME) Sir Henry Fowler introduced the 4-6-0 'Royal Scot' locomotives. His successor, Sir William Stanier, introduced new standardised locomotives and carriages, and in 1937 the streamlined 'Coronation Scot'. The LMS Anglo-Scottish service from London Euston bound for Carlisle and Glasgow Central, named the 'Royal Scot', traditionally departed Euston at 10 a.m. The LNER, with an equally famous CME, Sir Nigel Gresley, developed express locomotives, new carriages and the non-stop London–Edinburgh 'Flying Scotsman' service, followed by the 'Queen of Scots Pullman', then in 1935 the streamlined 'Silver Jubilee', and in 1937 the 'Coronation' and the 'West Riding Limited'. The LNER Scottish route ran from London King's Cross to Edinburgh Waverley; the 'Flying Scotsman' also departed at 10 a.m. Throughout this period, the LMS and LNER competed for prestigious speed records (in 1938 the LNER A4 Pacific *Mallard* achieved a speed of 126 mph, which remains a record for a steam locomotive). Both companies held the affections of the travelling public, offering a variety of different travel offers and special tickets on named trains to Scotland.

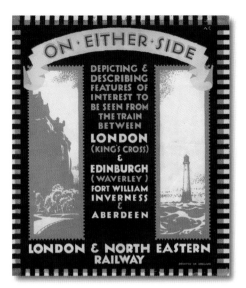

The cover of a seventy-six-page LNER publication entitled *On Either Side*.

LNER tickets from named express trains of the 1930s.

The 'Golden Arrow', the Southern's London to Paris express service.

BR's Southern Region carried on the Southern's 'Belle' tradition, introducing the 'Devon Belle' Pullman and observation car in June 1947 and the 'Kentish Belle' in 1951, which replaced the SR 'Thanet Belle'.

The Southern Railway, formed at the Grouping in 1923, was not to be outdone and offered prestigious Pullman express services – the 'Golden Arrow', the 'Brighton Belle' and the 'Bournemouth Belle' – and connections with cross-Channel services. The Southern operated its short sea service from London Victoria; the 'Golden Arrow' departed the terminus at 11 a.m. and arrived at Paris just before 6 p.m., using the Dover–Calais sea crossing. The 'Bournemouth Belle' Pullman service departed from Waterloo at 10.30 a.m.

The GWR company remained intact after the Grouping and continued its well-established tradition of high-speed express trains. This postcard view shows the company's advanced and highly successful 'Saint' class, hauling an express, c. 1906.

bound for Southampton West, Bournemouth Central and Bournemouth West. The one-hour 'Brighton Belle' service departed Victoria at 11 a.m.

The GWR named its express service to Plymouth the 'Cornish Riviera Limited' in 1905, building on the reputation of its earlier West Country express services the 'Flying Dutchman' and the 'Cornishman'. From 1935, the reintroduced 'Cornishman' service left Paddington at 10.35 a.m. for Penzance. Other named train services on the GWR were the 'Torbay Express' (for Torquay) and the 'Bristolian', while South Wales had the 'Tenby and Carmarthen Bay Express'. The express service between Paddington and Swindon was the 'Cheltenham Flyer', which held the record as the fastest train in the world up to 1935. The tickets from these companies' special express services tell a very special tale of upward mobility, glamour and prestige in an era of the high-speed steam train.

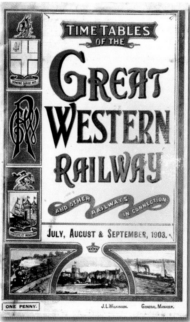

Left: The GWR timetable included main-line express services to Cornwall, Devon and Somerset, and to Wales via the Severn Tunnel.

Below: A GWR express ticket to Taunton.

49

Travel is subject to National Rail Conditions of Carriage (NRCoC) and to the conditions of carriage of other operators on whose services this ticket is valid. Copies of the NRCoC can be obtained from any staffed national rail station or from website: www.nationalrail.co.uk

Class	Ticket type	Adult	Child	
STD	OFF-PEAK DAY R	ONE	NIL	RTN
	Start date	Number		
	29·SEP·10	51171	5150458148	

From	Valid until	Price
BIRMINGHAM STNS	29·SEP·10	£5·90 M
To	Route	Validity
KIDDERMINSTER *	ANY PERMITTED	SEE RESTRICTNS

2-PART RETURN

Printed 10:22 on 29·SEP·10

MODERN TICKETS

THE MODERN TICKET provides the passenger with a receipt for the journey, authorises travel under a certain class and over a specified route, and ensures that the company receives its dues and no fraud takes place. The re-privatisation of the railways and the formation of train operating companies (TOCs) in 1996 did not change this, although a new organisation, the Association of Train Operating Companies (ATOC), with its division the Railways Settlement Plan (RSP), was formed to apportion each TOC its share of revenue on through routes.

The categories of ticket offered on the modern national railway network are not greatly different from those of the nineteenth and early twentieth centuries, and British TOCs have not changed ticketing practice greatly since the 1980s. The familiar credit-card-sized orange and yellow magnetic stripe tickets and the larger ATB2 style are provided to the train-operating companies under contract from ATOC. The main categories are first- and standard-class tickets. Anytime single or return tickets allow travel at any time, and permit a break in the journey. Off-peak tickets are valid on trains that are less busy, and sometimes there are 'super off-peak' fares, valid on the least busy services. Advance travel tickets are for specific trains – without a break in the journey – and booked at least a day and up to twelve weeks before travel. Season tickets give unlimited travel between two stations for a specified period. Railcards offer discounts on local journeys, or for people of specific age groups or in full-time education, for people aged sixty and above or with a disability, for adults travelling with children aged five to fifteen, for leisure travel in the London and south-east area, and for members of the armed forces. 'Rover' and 'Ranger' tickets offer flexible unlimited travel in a specified area. Some include bus and ferry services. Most train companies offer discounts for groups travelling together, and some offer 'GroupSave' tickets for three or four people travelling together to pay as two adults; both types are for off-peak journeys only. Travelcards allow unlimited travel on National Rail, London Underground, Docklands Light Railway and other integrated forms of

Opposite: Birmingham's Snow Hill station was rebuilt from scratch and reopened in 1987, ten years after the old GWR station was demolished, and fifteen years after rail services had ceased. London Midland now operates the station and shares platforms with Chiltern Railways and the Midland Metro.

transport for one day. 'Travelcard Season' tickets are also available.

Several new forms of ticketing are now appearing. Smart ticketing allows 'touch in, touch out' processing of a passenger's travel rights as it passes over a reader at a gate. The London Oyster Card system is a smart

The ticket window and booking hall are a familiar sight to all railway travellers, and one that has changed relatively little since the 1840s.

ticketing system that is expanding over the Greater London area. Another smart system uses ITSO (Integrated Transport Smartcard Organisation) cards similar to Oyster. They are intended to be used on all forms of public transport. Tickets are increasingly becoming available from self-service ticket machines at stations. The machines can also be used to

Above and left: The inspection of tickets on entering or leaving the platform is another familiar sight. The 'gate line' at Snow Hill station is fully automated but is occasionally staffed by a ticket examiner and revenue inspector.

An automated ticket-dispensing machine (far left) and a smart ticket reader (left), the alternative to the ticket window and ticket examiner.

53

collect tickets booked online or by telephone. Another source is a travel agent licensed to sell rail tickets. Through tickets are also available from selected British railway stations to Paris, Brussels and Lille by Eurostar or in partnership with European railway operators for destinations further into Europe.

The TOCs also impose penalty fares on some routes to deter fare evaders who fail to purchase a ticket from a station ticket office, self-service machine or online, or buy a permit to travel.

There has been a series of different formats of tickets since the introduction of APTIS in the mid-1980s and its gradual replacement by modern systems such as Tribute, Star, CRS smart cards and computer-generated travel documents. Various ticket formats are readily available on national railways, and many British heritage railways continue to use Edmondson card tickets. All railway-operating companies advertise and promote ticket deals, and for the price of the fare the collector can easily buy a British railway ticket. Tickets are available from high-speed rapid transit systems, the Channel Tunnel, garden and miniature railways, narrow-gauge

systems such as the Welsh Highland Railway (WHR), the Isle of Man, or for prestigious rail journeys such as 'Shakespeare's Express' and the 'Orient Express'. Commemorative ticket issues also celebrate former railway companies' lines, stations and anniversaries, and there are always railway events and tours.

Above and left: Some commemorative issues and tickets from preserved lines and stations.

Phone-card-sized tickets, and a souvenir ticket from the London Transport Underground.

COLLECTING RAILWAY TICKETS

BECAUSE BRITISH RAILWAY TICKETS are colourful, interesting and informative they make ideal objects to collect, and there are many potential themes for a collector, either geographic or historic. A collection might comprise a single ticket from a solitary station or any number of examples from a line, region or company. The collection might be of a narrow-gauge, broad-gauge or miniature railway, and the collection might be organised by the issuing station or arriving stations, or alphabetically, including exceptional, unusual, decorative or scarce tickets. A collection may also take up a theme and include different types and categories of ticket. Two obvious distinct forms of collecting are travel and platform tickets; each has a dedicated group of supporters and collectors. Like the postage stamp, the Edmondson ticket is conveniently sized (2 ¼ by 1 ¼ inches) and it is ideally suited for collecting, easily sorted and displayed in albums and plastic sleeves – as used by cigarette-card collectors – or mounted on card using self-adhesive transparent photograph corners. Non-Edmondson tickets, passes, paper tickets and modern credit-card-sized tickets are ideally displayed in plastic sleeves held in loose-leaf binders.

The theme of a collection is largely one of personal choice and affordability: some tickets are relatively inexpensive; others might cost hundreds of pounds, and, in some instances, thousands. A British railway ticket collection might comprise a 'stations' collection organised by receiving or issuing stations, perhaps based on a distinct period in British railway

Opposite:
Ways to store one's collection range from the narrow A4 box files shown for loose bundles of tickets, to several types of folders, some available with clear plastic inserts and individually formed pockets.

BRITISH RAILWAYS BOARD (M)   BR 4405/4

LLANFAIRPWLLGWYNGYLLGOGERYCHWYRNDROBWLLLLANTYSILIOGOGOGOCH

PLATFORM TICKET 3d.

AVAILABLE ONE HOUR ON DAY OF ISSUE ONLY
NOT VALID IN TRAINS NOT TRANSFERABLE
FOR CONDITIONS SEE OVER

21520   21520

1 2 3 4 5 6 7 8 9 10 11 12

Left This station near the Britannia Bridge has an unusually long name, often shortened to Llanfair PG.

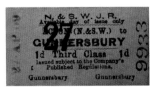

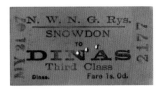

Some tickets to suggest a
collecting theme: narrow gauge,
pre-grouping companies or
regional railways.

history or representing a single company and district. Popular choices are pre-Grouping companies (before 1923), the 'Big Four', joint and independent lines, minor or miniature railways, BR regions, London's railways, and the LPTB and the Underground. A 'theme' collection might include article or animal tickets, or concentrate on a particular type or design of ticket; it might include commemorative and special-issue tickets. A specialised collection might illustrate interesting independent railways or a long-closed branch line. The Bishop's Castle Railway (see page 44) is such a line, along with its nearby neighbour the Shropshire & Montgomeryshire Railway – ideal subjects for a collection of lost lines, or as two railways in a county of Shropshire collection. Many small independent lines struggled to survive into the early part of the twentieth century; some started out with grandiose ideas for expansion, others were promoted by businessmen and landowners to serve local interests, but, as road transport increased, most succumbed to economic pressure. Many collectors are still fascinated by these largely forgotten small railways, and especially by the group of quirky railways brought together as 'Associated Railways', administered from Tonbridge by Colonel Holman Frederick Stephens (1868–1931). The colonel was also Engineer and Locomotive Superintendent of the Festiniog Railway and Welsh Highland Railway. The railways he is associated with are:

OWNED BY COLONEL STEPHENS
East Kent
Rother Valley (RVR), later KESR
Hundred of Manhood & Selsey Tramway (later WSR)
Kent & East Sussex (KESR)
Shropshire & Montgomeryshire (SMR)
West Sussex Light (WSLR)
Weston Clevedon & Portishead (WCPR)

MANAGED (MANAGING DIRECTOR OR ENGINEER)
Ashover Light
Burry Port & Gwendraeth Valley (BPGVR)
Edge Hill Light
North Devon & Cornwall Junction
Paddock Wood & Hawkhurst Railway
Plymouth Devonport & South Western Junction
Rye & Camber Tramway
Sheppey Light

Irish railways before 1922, or the railways of Northern Ireland, or the Northern Counties Committee (NCC), a Northern Ireland constituent of

A selection of tickets from lines that were associated with Colonel Holman Stephens.

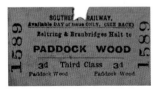

60

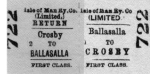

the LMS, might be worth collecting as part of a British Isles collection, although Ireland is a national collection in its own right. The Isle of Man railways offer another choice, with lines surviving from Victorian times; they include the Manx Northern Railway, the Peel line, the Port Erin line and the Snaefell Mountain Railway. Other island systems that could be collected are the railways of Jersey or those of the Isle of Wight. Private systems such as the Longmoor Military Railway (LMR), or the narrow-gauge railways of Wales, or regional railways serving a distinct region or conurbation are other possibilities. Private, independent, joint or large systems, national or regional, recently closed or still operational, are all suitable subjects for collectors.

These tickets are from island railways – the Isle of Man, the Isle of Wight and Jersey.

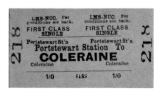

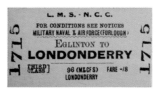

A selection of Northern Ireland railway tickets, comprising examples from the LMS Northern Counties Committee (LMSNCC), the Belfast & Northern Counties (BNCR), the County Donegal Railways Joint Committee (CDRJC) and the Londonderry & Lough Swilly Railway (LLSR).

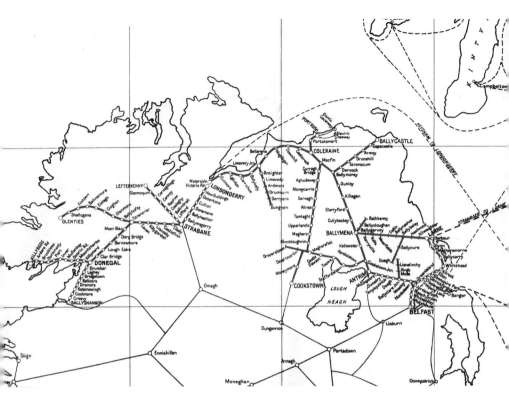

How to display the whole collection is partly dependent on space and available resources; large collections will take a lot of time and often cost a lot of money to manage and compile. The pleasure of tracking down and finding a suitable ticket is inevitably marred if that ticket cannot be displayed with the rest of a collection. Therefore arranging and displaying the collection is an important part of collecting; it follows that tickets can be displayed in combination with other items of ephemera, photographs, maps and diagrams to broaden the scope of a subject or theme. The display and care of tickets are largely the same thing, as a well-ordered collection is likely to lead to a well-looked-after collection. Here are some rules of thumb to help organise and maintain a collection.

Map of the railways of the north of Ireland.

- Conserve tickets, i.e. remove tickets from the worst effects of the environment and keep them out of strong light to reduce the risk of fading; keep them dry, flat, and free from dust and mechanical wear.
- Store large paper documents flat in acid-proof clear-fronted archive

63

paper bags, or a clear punched-hole document pouch held in a ring binder; support the document with card if necessary.

- Use card of 160–250 grams per square metre, with two diagonally opposite transparent photo corners to mount Edmondson tickets. The disadvantage here is that the back of the ticket cannot be seen, but the advantage is that the card can be pre-printed with information and descriptions; photographs and other ephemera can be included on the same card. The cards can be hole-punched and held in a loose-leaf binder. Care should be exercised if the ticket is to be removed: one photo corner should be split with a sharp knife to release the ticket – trying to pull out the ticket whole without removing a corner will inevitably lead to bending or creasing.

- Use four-ring plastic binders as they give more support to the card and mounted tickets, and less wear on the punched holes of the card.

- Alternatively use cigarette-card albums or phone-card albums. The plastic sheets and pouches are ideally suited to holding tickets, although tickets are prone to some movement in their individual pouches. Advantages are that the ticket can be examined from both sides and can be easily removed and organised. Take extra care when sliding the ticket into its pouch as it can be damaged on the edge of the plastic. Raise the plastic edge with tweezers and push the ticket into its pouch with the straight edge of a piece of card.

- Store albums in individual slipcases or partitions – it will further protect the albums from dust and damp.

- Index the collection and record at least the number and a brief description of each ticket by hand, or better still on a spreadsheet or database to aid security, and for the purpose of insurance indemnity. Even small collections can become more valuable over time.

- An alternative method is to scan the ticket using a flat-bed scanner, digital still or video camera and stand.

- Some cameras have live feed to a personal computer, which offers the opportunity to arrange tickets on the baseboard of the stand, before clicking the mouse button to capture the image.

- Similarly the camera memory chip is able to upload jpg, Raw or Tiff (for higher resolution) images to files on a computer; also back up and store copies on CD or DVD disks.

- Digital image file information is stored as metadata in the form of EXIF (Exchangeable Image File Format) or IPTC (International Press Telecommunications Council) standard. Some computer image software programmes allow additional information to be added to the image file metadata; the number and details of the ticket can therefore be added as a caption. Each image file then becomes a complete record of the ticket.

- Alternatively, name the file with the ticket number and company name, etc.
- Do not use any form of glue to paste tickets into an album, or, worse, sticky tape or staples.
- Do not use adhesive stamp hinges.
- Restoration will change the ticket physically and there is a high risk of damage in the attempt; even the removal of creases is a risky exercise.
- The removal of glue or contamination might be possible, but professional advice should be sought, and a little practice.
- Some remedial action is possible, such as the removal of old stamp hinges with stamp lift, but there are risks and it requires some prior experience.
- Never store albums in damp conditions and ensure that there is no mould present. Paper is prone to mycological attack and the ticket is composed of thin layers of paper pasted to two sides of a pasteboard substrate. The paper can detach in damp conditions and the ticket might bow.

One question a would-be collector of British railway tickets might ask is where to find and buy collectable tickets. Inevitably the next question is how and where to sell them, and how much are they worth. Every collectable

Paddington Ticket Auctions is a specialist auction house for collectors of British railway tickets.

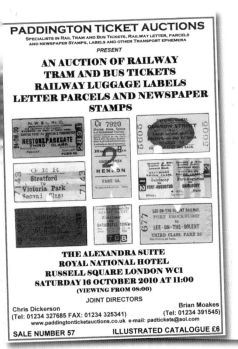

ticket has a monetary value, and some seemingly similar tickets issued from the same period or the same line fetch different prices; usually it is how rare and scarce a ticket is that dictates its price. Generally, the older pre-Grouping tickets are more valuable since they are rarer and there are fewer available on the market, but some pre-Grouping stations and companies issued many and so there are more available, and these tickets are therefore cheaper. Occasionally a chance find of a bundle of tickets increases the availability of certain types; it may also be that for whatever reason some companies held large stocks of unused tickets that were turned over to collectors when lines and stations closed. Another generalisation is that single-fare tickets are usually worth more than returns and halves, although a half ticket from an obscure station might be one of a very few such tickets in existence, in which case rival collectors may be keen to buy it at the first opportunity and to pay a good price. Issued tickets with provenance, post-dated tickets, audits, specimen tickets and the small number of spuriously dated tickets that surface occasionally are proportionally less valuable. When it comes to a valuation, it pays to do a little research, though a railway museum or library is unlikely to help. Many of these institutions actively discourage ad-hoc valuations and usually direct enquiries to auctioneers, but do email and contact them for advice. There is one specialist auction house, the Paddington Ticket Auctions, named after its original location near Paddington station, which specialises in rail, tram and bus tickets, railway letter, parcels and newspaper stamps, labels and other transport ephemera. Established railwayana auction houses offer occasional special auctions of tickets or include tickets with their normal railwayana lots.

A good organisation to contact for answers to questions on British railway tickets is the Transport Ticket Society (TTS). The Ticket and Fare Collection Society was originally founded in 1946, and in 1963 it teamed up with the International Society of Transport Ticket Collectors to form the TTS. Its members are mostly from the United Kingdom, and its interests include road, rail, airlines and shipping. The society's library holds a wide range of reference works on tickets and related subjects, and other activities include ticket exchange pools and postal auctions. The TTS publishes *The Journal of the Transport Ticket Society*, available to members, and advises on identifying, dating and valuing tickets, and on disposing of collections.

A well-looked-after collection will last a lifetime and probably outlive its collector. It is therefore advisable to make provisions for its future. Tickets have a monetary value and serious consideration should be given to bequeathing a collection to an institution or organisation. Libraries and museums should be made aware well in advance of a proposed bequest, and terms and conditions agreed. Many organisations are not able to take on the responsibility of looking after a large ticket collection and their interests might be better served if they are permitted to sell off parts of a collection to help fund other activities. Selling privately at a ticket auction or entering into a commissioned sale agreement with dealers is the alternative way of disposing of tickets, but it is most likely that a collection will be split up into lots for sale. However, it is possible to preserve the essence of a collection as data and images – a virtual collection – by scanning and digitising it on to DVD and PC hard drives.

Old used tickets and railcards often appear at railway preservation fund-raising shops amidst other forms of railway ephemera. Some shops also offer to buy stocks of tickets or sell them on commission. The other main source of old tickets is from railway swapmeets and specialist collectors' fairs. GBTicket organises

Right and below: The Transport Ticket Society publishes a monthly journal for members, covering a wide range of ticketing subjects.

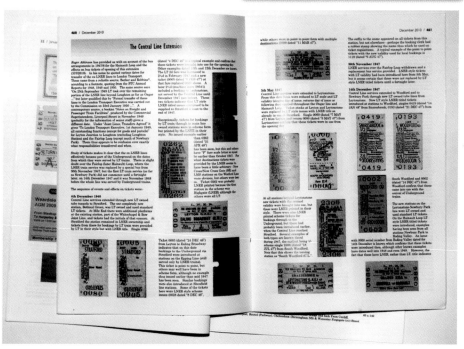

| Church | Mary | s hollow | White | Hazel | close to | the | Rapid | Whirlpool | Church | St. Tysilio | Cave | red |

LLANFAIRPWLLGWYNGYLLGOGERYCHWYRNDROBWLL-LLANTYSILIOGOGOGOCH.

THIS IS THE FULL NAME OF THE VILLAGE AND PARISH OF LLANFAIR, SITUATED NEAR MENAI BRIDGE. THE WORD IN ITS ENTIRETY IS NOT ORDINARILY USED BUT ABBREVIATED TO LLANFAIR P.G. ON ACCOUNT OF THE FACT THAT THERE ARE MANY OTHER VILLAGES OF THE SAME NAME THROUGHOUT WALES. IT IS NOT A DIFFICULT WORD TO PRONOUNCE AFTER MEMORISATION. THE MEANING OF THE PLACE NAME CONVEYS THAT IT IS THE PLACE OF ST. MARY'S CHURCH IN A DELL OF WHITE HAZEL TREES NEAR THE RAPID WHIRLPOOL NEAR WHICH WAS A RED CAVE AND THE CHURCH OF ST. TYSILIO. — Copyright

TUBULAR BRIDGE, LLANFAIR P. G.

Above: At one end of the collecting scale are tickets worth thousands of pounds. Britannia Bridge over the Menai Strait in Anglesey was engineered by Robert Stephenson and William Fairbairn and opened in 1851. The station at Britannia Bridge closed seven years after the bridge opened, and this ticket is the only one known, a rare and valuable find.

Right: Souvenir shops on preserved railways often sell old railway tickets. This one on the SVR at Hampton Loade station offers tickets for sale at just a few pence.

fairs in Birmingham and London offering facilities to a range of traders, and publishes its own online transport ticket catalogue. Other sales are through eBay, and a number of bespoke and specialist collectors' lists are available to the collector on application. Their names and addresses can be found from talking to collectors and stallholders at auctions and ticket fairs. Georgemas Junction offers a general list of moderately priced tickets ideally suited for the beginner, and Mike Freeman's list caters for a wide range both of moderately priced and of higher-priced rare tickets.

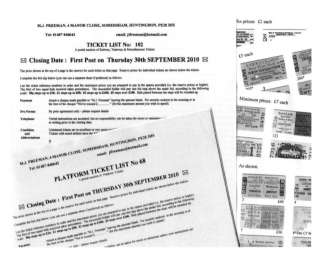

Mike Freeman's postal auction lists and sales for the armchair collector are highly regarded.

GBTicket caters for internet ticket sales and collectors' fairs.

FURTHER INFORMATION

SUGGESTED READING

Awdry, Christopher. *Encyclopaedia of British Railway Companies*. Guild Publishing, 1990.

Bett, Wingate H. *The Theory of Fare Collection on Railways and Tramways*. W. J. Fowler & Sons Ltd, 1945.

Cobb, Colonel M. H. *The Railways of Great Britain, A Historical Atlas* (volumes 1 and 2). Ian Allan Publishing, 2003.

Fairchild, G., and Wootton, P. *Railway and Tramway Tickets*. Ian Allan Ltd, 1987.

Farr, Michael. *Thomas Edmondson and His Tickets*. Andover, 1991.

Geldard, D. G. *The First Fifty Years: The Early Development of the Railway Ticket*. Transport Ticket Society, 1984.

Geldard, D. G. *Edmondson Tickets of the North London Railway and Associated Companies*. Transport Ticket Society, 2001.

Geldard, D. G. *Ordinary Single and Return Tickets of the Midland Railway*. Solo Publication, 2008.

Geldard, D. G. *Ordinary Single and Return Tickets of the GWR Prior to 1923*. Solo Publication, 2004.

Geldard, D. G. *Ordinary Single and Return Tickets of the South Eastern Railway, London, Chatham & Dover Railway and South Eastern & Chatham Railway* (volume 1). Solo Publication, 2006.

Geldard, D. G. *Ordinary Single and Return Tickets of the South Eastern Railway and London Chatham & Dover Railway and South Eastern Dover & Chatham Railway* (volume 2). Solo Publication, 2007.

Lee, Charles E. *Passenger Class Distinctions*. London Railway Gazette, 1946.

Quick, Michael E. *A Chronology of Railway Passenger Stations in Great Britain*. Railway & Canal Historical Society, 2009.

Stewart, M. G. *British Platform Tickets to 1948*. Transport Ticket Society, 1986.

Wiener, Lionel. *Passenger Tickets*. The Railway Gazette, 1940.

Williams, Frederick S. *Our Iron Roads, Their History, Construction and Administration*. Bemrose & Sons, 1883.

Williams, Frederick S. *The Midland Railway*. Bemrose & Sons, 1877.

Talking Tickets Magazine, edited by Brian Pask. Available by subscription from the publisher, Bestchart Limited, 6A Mays Yard, Down Road, Waterlooville, Hants PO8 0YP. Email: info@bestchart.co.uk Telephone: 023 9259 7707.
The Journal of the Transport Ticket Society (published monthly), edited by David Harman (managing editor), Transport Ticket Society.

TICKET CONTACTS AND WEB ADDRESSES

ORGANISATIONS
Association of Train Operating Companies: www.atoc.org Telephone enquiries: 0207 841 8000.
Central Library, Birmingham, Social Sciences – The Wingate Bett Transport Ticket Collection: www.birmingham.gov.uk/libraries
London Midland Trains: www.londonmidland.com
National Railway Museum,York, Search Engine: www.nrm.org.uk/researchandarchive
John Rylands University Library, Manchester: Edmondson Ticket Collection (Edmondson tickets)
Transport Ticket Society: www.transport-ticket.org.uk

BUYING AND SELLING TICKETS
M. J. Freeman, Postal Auction Catalogue, 4 Manor Close, Somersham, Huntingdon PE28 3HS. Email: jifreeman@hotmail.com
Georgemas Junction, Postal Auction Catalogue, 16 Williams Close, Longwell Green, South Gloucestershire BS30 9BS. Email: mark.bladwell@btinternet.com
GB Tickets, Online Transport Ticket Catalogue: www.gbticket.co.uk Email: gbticket@gbticket.co.uk
Paddington Ticket Auctions: www.paddingtonticketauctions.co.uk Email: padtickets@aol.com

INDEX

Illustrations are shown in italic type